Phonemic Awareness

Listening Activities to Develop Pre-Reading Skills

Grades K-2

by

Hildi Kang

Published by Fearon Teacher Aids
an imprint of
Frank Schaffer Publications®

Author: Hildi Kang
Editors: Lisa Trumbauer, Lisa Schwimmer Marier
Cover and Interior Design: Rose Sheifer Graphic Productions

Frank Schaffer Publications®

Fearon Teacher Aids is an imprint of Frank Schaffer Publications.

Send all inquiries to:
Frank Schaffer Publications
3195 Wilson Drive NW
Grand Rapids, Michigan 49544

Phonemic Awareness—grades K-2

ISBN: 1-56417-944-3

6 7 8 9 10 11 MAL 09 08 07 06 05

CONTENTS

INTRODUCTION

Welcome to *Phonemic Awareness*—a somewhat new, somewhat confusing term. To define what phonemic awareness is, let's start with what it is **not.**

- Phonemic awareness is **not** reading.
- It does **not** deal with alphabet letters.
- It is **not** phonics.
- It does **not** replace your reading program.
- It is **not** an all-out cure for reading problems.

What Is Phonemic Awareness?

So what *is* phonemic awareness? Phonemic awareness is recognizing sounds within words.

Phonemic awareness is the official name given for oral language and auditory discrimination skills you probably practiced and sharpened in your own childhood. For example, perhaps you chanted nonsense rhymes, such as "hickory dickory dock." Or, perhaps a friend spoke to you in a special language, like "Ut-way rr-ay oo-yay ooing-day ooday-tay?" (What are you doing today?) If so, you were phonemically aware without even knowing it. You understood that words are made up of distinct sounds and that these sounds can be separated.

In the "Developmental Progression of Phonological Segmentation Skills" seminar at a Learning Disabilities Association of America conference, Corinne Smith listed the sounds most children recognize spontaneously.

In preschool (ages 3-4), children can:

- recognize a babble nonsense rhyme when given a clue.
- detect rhymes by the ages of 3 and 4.

In kindergarten (ages 4-5), many children can:

- group words together based on rhyme.
- answer correctly when asked if two words rhyme.
- distinguish if two words begin with the same sound or end with the same sound.
- segment words into syllables.
- blend sounds to form words (d - o - g = dog, m - an = man).

In grade one (ages 6-7), children can:

- break a dictated word into syllables.
- delete the initial phoneme and repeat the word without the beginning sound.

Again, these listening and oral skills come naturally for most children.

Why Teach Phonemic Awareness?

Researchers now know that such skills as rhyming, hearing initial sounds, and blending sounds together, are the building blocks for reading. Good readers do these things intuitively.

Researchers have also found that when these skills are introduced randomly, or embedded in a larger lesson, the only children who respond are the ones who already possess the skills. Those who don't possess the skills—children who need it the most—either mimic the skills or don't respond at all. To reach those children, these skills must be specifically taught.

When Should I Teach Phonemic Awareness?

Phonemic awareness can be taught as early as kindergarten. Throughout kindergarten and into grade 1, introduce the skills to all children. Continue phonemic awareness in grades 2 and 3 with those children who remain weak in reading.

When teaching phonemic awareness, there are several key points to keep in mind:

- Skills should be taught in specific lessons.
- You should try to practice phonemic awareness about 10 to 15 minutes a day, three or four times a week.
- The more consistent your lesson structure, the more improvement you will observe in your young learners.
- As you get to know the children's skills, regroup them. Put those who are successful in phonemic awareness together and sustain their skills with lessons once a week.

The Four Skills of Phonemic Awareness

Phonemic awareness is broken down into four basic skills.

- **Rhyming Sounds:** Children can hear and recognize that the last part of some words sound the same.
- **Blending Sounds:** Children can hear and recognize individual sounds in words—for example, *c -at* or *c-a-t*.
- **Matching Sounds:** Children can hear and recognize words with the same initial sound and words with the same ending sound.
- **Segmenting Sounds:** Children can hear a word and clap the number of syllables. Or, children can repeat a word, then leave part of the word out.

How to Teach Phonemic Awareness

Phonemic awareness is most effective when you work with a small group of children—about five or six. All four skills are best done in tandem, one after the other in short daily lessons, using a few examples of each. However, sometimes shifting skills within a lesson confuses children. Use your best judgment. Work on one or two skills at a time, depending on the needs of your group. As children become comfortable with one skill, add another.

To begin practice for each skill, say a word or show a picture to the group, and ask for a response. For example, you might start with the word *cat*. Invite children to come up with words that ***rhyme*** with *cat*, such as *bat, hat, mat, fat,* and *sat.* You might continue by helping children separate the word into individual sounds (c-a-t) to hone ***blending***. Practice ***matching*** skills by asking children to come up with words that have the same beginning sound (*cake, count, color*) and then ask children to clap the syllables (***segment***).

On subsequent lessons, increase the difficulty. Present children with two pictures, and challenge them to choose the item that rhymes. For example, for the word *cat,* you might show children a picture of a bat and a picture of a ball. Which is the rhyming word? When they understand the task, increase the choice to three pictures. As children approach mastery, challenge them to choose the rhyming word from up to ten pictures.

How to Use This Book

This book has been divided into four sections, one for each skill. Each skill has one page of instruction, followed by supplementary activities. Do not consider one skill to be more difficult than another, for children have their own individual strengths and weaknesses. One child may be good at one skill while unable to do another. Other children might have responses that are completely different.

Please be aware that within each skill area, there are different levels of difficulty. The first activity on a page will be the easiest. The activities will then become more difficult as you progress down the page. Your own observations of children's responses will tell you when to continue on to more difficult tasks.

But what happens if you have a child who simply cannot give you a rhyming word, for example, or find two words that begin with the same sound? How do you teach these children? Here are four suggestions for teaching children with weak auditory skills. (Note: If these strategies do not help, the child might have a specific learning disability. Check with your school speech therapist or resource specialist.)

1. FEEL

Have the child feel the motion and position of lips and mouth as the sounds are produced. This gives the sounds a new dimension and provides additional feedback to the brain. For example, ask the child to place a hand lightly on his or her throat to feel the vibration of the *m* sound (/m/). Or, have the child place a hand in front of his or her mouth to feel the puff of air with the *p* sound (/p/). Or, have the child feel how his or her lips bump together to form the *b* sound (/b/).

2. DESCRIBE

Have the child describe the articulation of sounds. What does the child actually feel happening to the mouth, tongue, and throat? If two words rhyme, for example, the child should feel the same sensation with each word.

3. WATCH

Have the child watch you say the word and then mimic your oral movements.

4. MAKE THE SOUND TANGIBLE

If a child cannot get the idea of a sound, take an appealing object, like a toy dinosaur or a bear math counter, and relate it to the sound. For example:

Say to the child "When we say the word *mop*, do you hear the *-op* sound at the end? This bear will be the *-op* sound.

Say *"mm-op"* and touch the bear as you say the *"-op"* sound.

Touch the bear again, and ask the child, "What sound is the bear?"

(-op)

Say a non-rhyming word, like *ss-at,* and ask "Do you hear the *-op*?" (Do not touch the bear.)

Say a rhyming word, like *top*, and ask "Do you hear the *-op*?" (Touch the bear.)

The activities in this book use phonemic awareness. You are encouraging children to become aware of and sharpen skills they already have or have the ability to develop. For most children, practice will make perfect.

Assessment

Try this method to keep track of children's progress. Make a chart for each group of children. Write the four phonemic activities across the top, and list children's names down the left side.

	rhyme	blend	match	segment
Darren	+++0+++	+++++++	00+0++++	+00+++
Sharmay	000+0000	++0++00+	0+000+00	00++0++

During a lesson, listen and observe the child's responses. If the child can successfully complete the skill, write a "+" in the box. If not, write a "0." It is then easy to see at a glance whether a child has the skill, is gradually acquiring the skill, or needs more practice.

REMINDERS

Keep these points in mind when practicing both phonemic awareness and applying the activities in this book:

- Tasks vary in their difficulty.
- Tasks with multiple syllables are usually easier to grasp than those with single-syllable words.
- Initial consonants are easier to work with than final consonants.
- Letter sounds that can be sustained, or drawn out, such as vowels and the consonants *f, l, m, n, r, s, v,* and *z,* are easier to work with than ones that cannot be sustained, such as *b, c, t,* and *p,* for example.
- Before using a lesson with a group, practice saying the letter sounds so that you do not put "uh" after the consonants.

  Say **/ssss/**, not **/suh/**.

  Say **/mmm/**, not **/muh/**.

  Try to say **/b/**, not **/buh/** and **/t/**, not **/tuh/**, although these are more difficult.

(Note: When you see / / around a letter, it indicates that the ***sound*** *should be said, not the name of the letter.)*

References and Acknowledgments

RESEARCH

All activities are based on the following:

1. E. W. Ball and B. A. Blachman, "Phoneme Segmentation Training: Effect on Reading Readiness." *Annals of Dyslexia,* Vol. 38, Pages 208-25, 1988, and "Does Phoneme Awareness Training in Kindergarten Make a Difference in Early Word Recognition and Developmental Spelling?" *Reading Research Quarterly,* Vol. 26 (1), Pages 49-66, 1991.
2. L. Bradley and P. Bryant, "Categorizing Sounds and Learning to Read: A Causal Connection." *Nature,* Vol. 30, Pages 419-21, 1983, and *Rhyme and Reason in Reading and Spelling.* University of Michigan Press, 1985.
3. A. E. Cunningham, "Explicit vs. Implicit Instruction in Phonemic Awareness." *Journal of Experimental Child Psychology,* Vol. 50(3), Pages 429-44, 1990.
4. I. Lundberg, J. Frost, and O. Peterson, "Effects of an Extensive Program for Stimulating Phonological Awareness in Preschool Children." *Reading Research Quarterly,* Vol. 23 (3), Pages 263-84, 1988.

ACKNOWLEDGMENTS

Pictures

Grateful acknowledgment is made to the Berkeley Unified School District for permission to reprint adaptations of rhyming pictures from *Word Study Instructional Materials Guide* by Pat Endsley and Amy Snodgrass. Berkeley Unified School District, Berkeley, CA, 1977.

The author also gratefully acknowledges useful discussions with Holly Massey, Speech Therapist, Livermore School District.

ONE LAST POINT

Research on phonemic awareness as a primary factor in dyslexia is extremely strong and teachers must be trained to appreciate its significance in teaching all beginning readers. There is a need for specialized procedures, such as the Lindamood Auditory Discrimination in Depth Program, or Benita Blachman's beginning reading program, both of which are being studied in National Institute for Child Health and Human Development research. These programs directly develop phonemic awareness and should be used prior to and in combination with phonics instruction.

—Dr. Reid Lyon, psychologist with the Human Learning and Behavior branch of the National Institutes of Health
Network News Bulletin, Lindamood-Bell Research and Training Network, San Luis Obispo, CA , p. 4, August, 1995.

MATERIALS

- ✓ The word list on pages 22–23 (rhyming words)
- ✓ Rhyming picture cards from pages 34–35
- ✓ Rhyming couplets activity sheet, page 12
- ✓ Game instructions, pages 13–15

SKILL 1

Rhyming Sounds

OBJECTIVES:
- Children will be able to recognize rhyming words in isolation and in poetic couplets.
- Children will be able to make rhyming words in response to a target word.

Recognize the concept of rhyme

- Present two words or two pictures, and ask children if the two words rhyme. For example, show children a picture of a bat and a cat. Do these words have a similar sound? Yes. So they rhyme.
- Present children with two words that don't rhyme. Begin with words that are completely different, such as *cat* and *jump*. Gradually choose words that are more similar, yet still don't rhyme, such as *cat* and *jet*.
- Always be sure to ask one child at a time to respond so no one child dominates the activity.

Supply a rhyming word

- Say a word, such as *cat*. Then challenge each child in the group to come up with a word that rhymes with the word *cat*. Accept all words, real or nonsense, as long as they rhyme. Write the children's words on the chalkboard or on chart paper to help them start making the association between the spoken word and the written word.
- Then read the rhyming couplets back to the group, such as *cat, sat*. Can children think of any rhymes they might have missed? Encourage children to suggest any other rhyming words. Again, accept any words that rhyme.
- When the group understands the concept of rhyme, it is time to try the next round of activities.

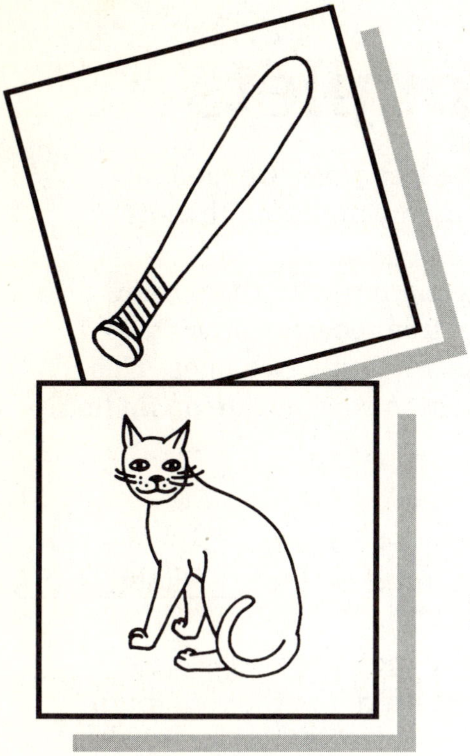

Choose the matching rhyme

- Display two pictures for everyone in the group to see. Say a word that rhymes with one of the pictures, and challenge a child to choose the picture with which it rhymes. For example, if you show children pictures of a cat and a ball, say the word *bat*. Which picture rhymes with *bat? (Cat)*
- As children become more proficient in the skill, challenge them to find the rhyming picture among three or four picture choices.

Rhyming games

- Try playing the rhyming games as described on pages 13-15.
  Odd Man Out
  Concentration
  Bingo

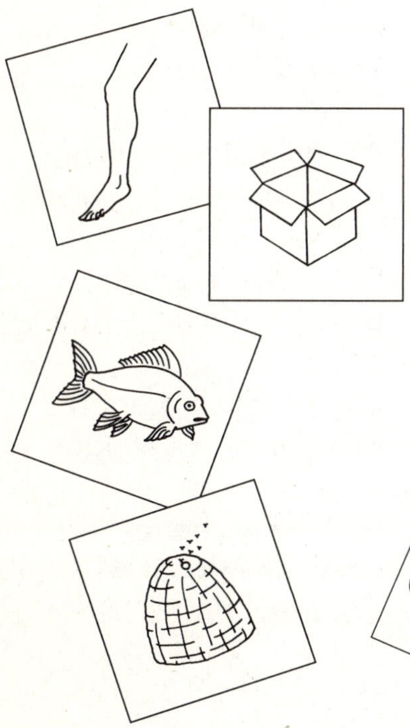

SKILL 1

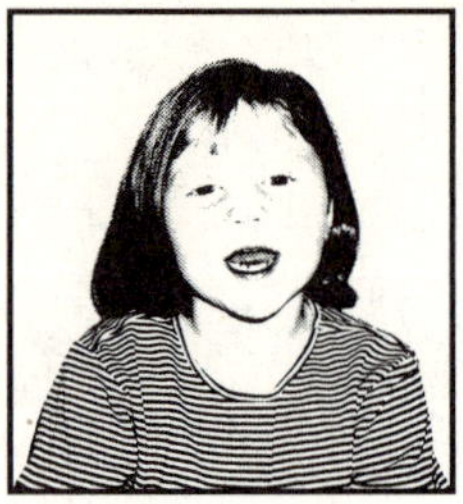

Rhyming Couplets

Read each couplet aloud, leaving out the last word. Challenge children to fill in the rhyming word. Accept any appropriate word that rhymes.

Invite children to hear other rhymes by sharing with them traditional Mother Goose rhymes or any others from poetry anthologies you have. Try to limit your poems to those with only two lines. This will focus children's attention, helping them to concentrate on finding the rhyme.

The dog sat alone,
watching his ___(bone)___.

The cat chased the mouse,
all around the ___(house)___.

I had a duck,
that rode in a ___(truck)___.

The giant took a rocket,
and put it in his ___(pocket)___.

The girl came back,
to get her ___(snack)___.

A boy took a map,
and put it in his ___(cap)___.

The funny little chicks,
did lots of ___(tricks)___.

Once there were some goats,
who ate up all the ___(coats)___.

Very late at night,
she turned on the ___(light)___.

Bobby took the flag,
and stuffed it in the ___(bag)___.

The car came to a stop,
in front of the old ___(shop)___.

Right behind the clock,
I found the missing ___(sock)___.

A family of little mice,
played on the ___(ice)___.

Sally rode in a train,
but never in a ___(plane)___.

Once I saw a dragon,
riding in a ___(wagon)___.

He hurt his head,
when he fell out of ___(bed)___.

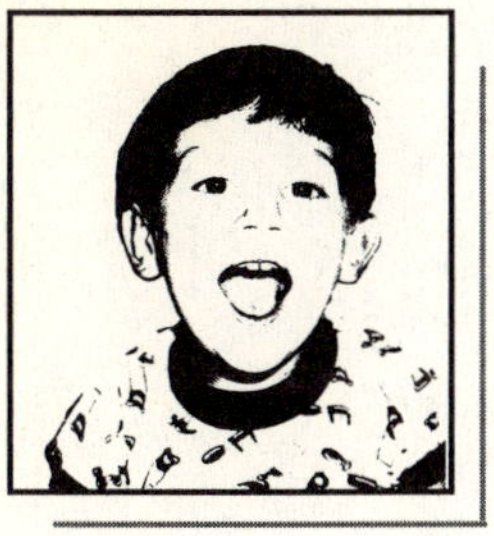

SKILL 1

Odd Man Out

Choose a picture strip from the picture cards (pages 36–45) at the end of this book. The strip should contain four pictures. You might take two pieces of construction paper, and put one above and one below the strip, revealing only the strip you wish to work with. This will avoid confusion and focus children's attention on only those pictures. In each strip, you will have two pictures that rhyme, two pictures with matching initial consonants, and probably two pictures with the same final consonant.

Show the picture strip to children and ask them to identify each picture. Have them listen closely to the sounds they make as they say each word. Then ask the following questions to elicit which words rhyme, which words have the same beginning sounds, and which words have the same ending sounds. For example:

Ask these questions:		**Which words are the "odd man out?"**
Which words rhyme?	fish, dish	fox and brush are out
Which words begin with the same sound?	fish, fox	dish and brush are out
Which words end with the same sound?	fish, dish, brush	fox is out

SKILL 1

Concentration

MATERIALS

✓ Rhyming picture cards on pages 34 and 35

ABOUT CONCENTRATION:

Concentration is best when played in small groups. This game follows the same rules as Concentration or Memory, except children are encouraged to recognize and remember pairs of rhyming words rather than identical words. For example, if a player turns over a card with a *cat,* he or she isn't looking for another *cat,* but a word that rhymes with *cat,* such as *bat.*

To begin play:

1. Shuffle the picture cards and spread them out, face down, on the table.
2. Instruct players to take turns turning over cards, two at a time.
3. Ask the player to say the words pictured on each card. Can the player hear if the words rhyme?
4. If the words pictured rhyme, the player removes the cards from the table and takes another turn.
5. If the words pictured do not rhyme, the player turns the cards back over, and it is the next player's turn.
6. The game ends when all the picture cards have been removed.
7. Instruct children to count their cards. The player with the most cards is the winner.

ALTERNATE IDEAS:

Use the rhyming picture cards (on pages 34–35) in other creative ways as well. Here are two alternate rhyming games to try with the group.

- Place all the picture cards in a pile, face down. Invite each child to turn over a card and to come up with his or her own rhyming word. For example, if the child turns over the *cat,* he or she might say "Hat."
- Separate the picture cards into two rhyming stacks. Keep one stack for yourself, and give one stack to the group. Have the group members pass out the cards among themselves so each child has one or more picture cards, depending on the size of the group. Turn over one card in your stack. Invite the child who has the rhyming word to show the group the card, asking the other children to confirm that it rhymes. The child then takes your card and couples it with the group's card to make a rhyming set. After all the cards have been paired, review the matches to make sure they all rhyme.

SKILL 1

Bingo

MATERIALS

- ✓ "Bingo" game board for each child, page 46.
- ✓ Two or three sets of rhyming picture cards, pages 34 and 35
- ✓ Markers, such as squares of construction paper, tokens, or plastic chips

SET-UP:

- Randomly paste one of each rhyming pair onto the spaces of the game boards. Each board should have the picture cards in different places on the board.
- If possible, laminate the boards.
- Prepare an additional set of game boards on which are pasted the remaining pictures from each rhyming pair.
- Mark this board "caller," and use it to call out the rhyming words during the game. Place a marker on each picture called.
- Prepare markers to cover the squares during play, such as small squares of construction paper, tokens, or plastic chips.

TO BEGIN PLAY:

1. Give each child a game board and markers.
2. Read the words pictured on the "caller" board.
3. Challenge players to search their game boards for a picture of a rhyming word. If they find a rhyming word, tell them to cover the picture with a marker.
4. Continue until someone calls out "Bingo!" This player will be the first child to completely cover a row of squares in any direction—across or down. Or, you might choose to play until players cover an entire game board.
5. The player who has "Bingo!" is the winner.

SKILL 2

Blending Sounds

MATERIALS

- ✓ The word list on pages 24–25 (blending sounds)
- ✓ The picture cards from pages 36–45
- ✓ Puppet activity, page 17

OBJECTIVES:
- As you stretch out sounds in a word, children will be able to recognize the individual sounds.
- Children will be able to blend sounds together to form words.

Stretch sounds in words

- Say a word, stretching out the sound of each letter or syllable as you say it. Some refer to this as "singing" when a word is slowed down.
- Others use a rubberband, stretching it as they say "I am going to s-t-r-e-t-c-h out a word, just like I'm stretching this rubberband. I want you to try and pop the word back together." (Relax the rubberband.)

Blend sounds into words

- Say a word, and pause between its sounds. For example, "/c/-/at/." Challenge children to blend the sounds into one word. (Remember to say /c/, not /cuh/.)
- Say the word again slowly. Ask children to listen closely, then say the word quickly.
- You might begin the lesson with familiar words, such as children's first names or objects around the room. When children become familiar with the procedure, move on to other words.
- When children approach mastery, break the words into more sounds: /c/-/a/-/t/.

Four ways to practice this skill:

- Say the words orally.
- Show the children two picture cards, and pronounce only one of the words. Have children point to the correct picture card.
- Continue with three or more picture cards.
- Try the puppet activity on page 17.

SKILL 2

Puppet Play

MATERIALS

✓ Puppet

✓ Storybook

To begin play:

1. Show children a puppet they all enjoy. Explain that this puppet is learning to read, but it has trouble reading some words.
2. Tell the group that the puppet is going to read them a story. Ask children to listen closely for the moments when the puppet has trouble reading.
3. Now open a book for the puppet to read to the class. As you read, randomly choose words to break into blends, saying the initial sound, then pausing before the rest of the word.
4. At this point, the puppet will turn away or hide its face, indicating that this is a word it can't read. Children must then blend the word together.
5. When they do, the puppet will turn around and continue the story.

MATERIALS

- ✓ The picture cards from pages 36–45
- ✓ Game instructions for "Odd Man Out" and "Concentration," pages 13 and 14

SKILL 3

Matching Sounds

OBJECTIVES:
- Children will recognize and distinguish same sounds at the beginning of words.
- Children will recognize and distinguish same sounds at the end of words.

Match initial sounds

- Show children two picture word cards, and invite them to say the words. Then say a word that begins with the same sound as one of the pictures. Challenge children to choose the correct picture. For example, you might show children pictures of a *cat* and a *ball*. Say the word *cake*. Guide children to match the initial sound in *cake* with the initial sound in *cat.*
- Try the activity again, only this time have children select from three or four picture cards.
- Say a word like *ball*. Brainstorm with children all the words they can think of that have the same beginning sound, such as *bike, balloon, bad, bed, box, boy, bell, basket*, and so on. You might write children's words on the chalkboard or on chart paper so they may make the connection between the spoken word and the written word. Point out that the beginning letter of each word is the same.

Match ending sounds

- Follow the above directions, but this time have children match ending sounds. For example, show children pictures of a *cat* and a *ball.* Then say the word *jet.* Help children match the ending sound of *jet* with the ending sound of *cat.*

Blending Games

- Invite children to play "Odd Man Out," just as they did for rhyming words. This time, however, ask them to match beginning and ending consonants.
- Children can also match beginning consonants during a game of "Concentration."

SKILL 4

Segmenting Sounds

OBJECTIVES:
- Children will be able to separate words into individual syllables.
- Children will be able to recognize specific sounds within words.

MATERIALS

- ✓ The word lists on pages 26–31
- ✓ The picture cards from pages 36–45
- ✓ Activity sheet on page 47
- ✓ Game instructions, page 20

Segment words into syllables

- Say a simple word, and invite children to clap how many syllables they hear. For example, if you say the word *cat*, children should clap once. Do not separate the word into its individual phonemes. Say it normally for children to clap to.
- Have children clap the number of syllables in a compound word. For example, if you say the word *cowboy*, children should clap twice.
- Say the compound word again for children to repeat.
- Then challenge children to say the compound word without one of the syllables, for example, "Say *cowboy* without *cow*." Children should be able to hear the word *boy* and repeat it.

Segment a word into its sounds

- Reproduce and pass out the activity sheet on page 47. Give children at least five beans or tokens to place on the sheet.
- Now say a word slowly, emphasizing each individual sound. For example, if the word is *clown*, say it as, "C-L-OW-N." How many different sounds do children hear? (They should hear four.) Have them move a bean down the page to the corresponding number.
- Give children picture cards. Ask them to sound out the words to themselves, then place their beans on the proper place on the activity sheet for you to check. This is often a more difficult task, for children must listen to their own pronunciations.

Deleting sounds in words

- Say a word like *cat*. Ask children to repeat it. Now ask children to delete the beginning sound. Can they say the word without the *c*? Challenge children to hear and say the word *at*. Try it with other words as well.
- Now try it with ending sounds. Again say *cat*, but ask children to remove the *t* sound at the end. Can children say the new word? They should respond with *ca*.

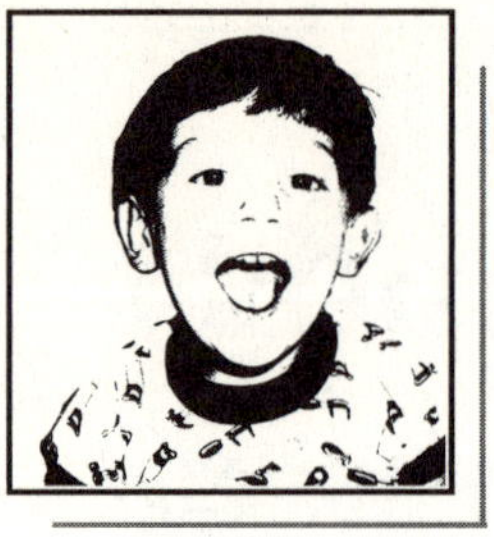

SKILL 4

Segmentation game

What Word Is Left?

Invite children to play this listening game. Present children with a word. Explain that if they take away the first letter sound, they actually create a new word. Invite children to try it. Start with this sample:

1. Say to the group "I am going to say a word. Listen closely! You must take off the first sound and say the new word."
2. Say the word *cat* and ask children to repeat the word.
3. Say the word again, but this time leave off the /c/ sound. Ask children to repeat the new word. What word do they hear?
4. Confirm children's responses. "You are right! The new word is *at!*"

Here are some other words to try:

- ice (mice, dice)
- is (his)
- age (cage, page, wage)
- old (bold, cold, fold, gold, hold, mold)
- ace (face, lace, pace)
- ox (fox, box)
- it (hit, bit, sit, pit, quit)
- all (ball, call, fall, mall)
- ear (hear, gear, fear, near)
- eat (heat, beat, seat, meat, neat)
- and (sand, hand, land, band, stand)
- or (for, nor)
- ill (bill, fill, pill)
- ail (sail, pail, rail, nail)
- end (bend, send, mend, trend)
- in (fin, pin, win, sin)
- out (pout, shout, bout, scout)

For more ideas, check the word list on pages 22 and 23.

APPENDIX

MATERIALS

✓ Words Lists

✓ Picture Cards

✓ Activity Sheets

Rhyming Words

The phonograms and rhyming words listed on these two pages are among the most common.

-ack:	back, jack, pack, rack, sack, black, crack, smack, snack, quack, track
-ain:	gain, main, rain, brain, drain, chain, train, stain
-ake:	bake, cake, lake, make, rake, sake, take, wake, snake, brake, shake
-ale:	bale, male, pale, tale, scale, whale
-all:	ball, call, fall, hall, mall, tall, wall, small
-am:	ham, jam, ram, clam, slam, cram
-ame:	came, fame, game, lame, name, same, tame, blame, flame, frame, shame
-an:	ban, can, fan, man, pan, ran, van, scan
-ank:	bank, sank, tank, crank, blank, thank, spank, plank
-at:	bat, cat, fat, hat, mat, pat, rat, vat, that, flat, chat
-ate:	date, gate, hate, late, rate, crate, state
-eat:	beat, feat, heat, meat, seat, cheat, treat
-ell:	bell, fell, sell, shell, smell, spell, swell
-est:	best, jest, nest, pest, test, rest, chest
-ice:	dice, lice, mice, nice, price, slice, twice
-ick:	lick, pick, sick, tick, quick, flick, click, slick, brick, trick, chick, stick
-ide:	hide, ride, side, tide, glide, slide, pride
-ight:	fight, light, might, night, right, sight, bright, fright, flight
-ike:	bike, hike, like, mike, spike, strike

Rhyming Words

-ill:	bill, fill, hill, pill, will, chill, spill, still
-in:	bin, fin, kin, pin, tin, chin, grin, spin
-ine:	dine, fine, mine, pine, wine, shine, nine
-ing:	ding, king, ring, bring, cling, swing
-ink:	link, mink, wink, pink, drink, think
-ip:	dip, hip, rip, chip, flip, drip, trip, skip
-ire:	fire, hire, tire, wire, spire
-ock:	dock, lock, sock, rock, block, shock
-oke:	joke, woke, broke, smoke
-op:	cop, hop, mop, chop, shop, stop
-ore:	bore, more, sore, tore, wore, store
-out:	bout, scout, spout, shout, trout, pout
-uck:	duck, luck, puck, tuck, stuck, truck
-ug:	bug, hug, mug, rug, plug, snug
-ump:	bump, jump, lump, pump, grump
-unk:	bunk, junk, sunk, chunk, skunk
-ush:	hush, rush, blush, crush, flush
-ust:	dust, just, must, rust, crust, trust

Blending Sounds

Present these words orally, pausing a half second between phonemes.
Invite children to tell you what the word is.

Two-phoneme Words: Consonant + ending

- b — all
- b — oom
- b — ug
- ch — uck
- d — oor
- ea — ch
- f — ame
- r — at
- h — elp
- j — azz
- k — ite

- b — at
- b — ounce
- c — ake
- c — ow
- d — ad
- t — eeth
- f — ix
- g — old
- h — op
- i — ce
- l — ight

- b — an
- b — ore
- c — at
- c — ome
- d — ime
- f — ast
- g — ame
- r — ead
- h — ike
- k — ick
- l — ake

- b — ill
- b — unch
- ch — ug
- c — ool
- d — eep
- f — at
- g — ood
- h — ay
- j — ump
- k — ing
- l — amp

Blending Sounds

Present these words orally, pausing a half second between phonemes.
Invite children to tell you what the word is.

Three-phoneme Words: Consonant + vowel sound + ending consonant

b — a — ck
c — oa — t
d — u — ck
h — ou — se
d — i — sh
b — oo — m
ch — u — ck
d — oo — r
k — i — te
m — ai — d

h — ea — d
f — o — x
c — a — ke
d — a — d
g — o — ld
h — o — p
l — i — ght
n — e — ck
b — o — x
p — a — ck

f — a — st
g — a — me
f — i — sh
h — i — ke
l — a — ke
th — u — mb
n — i — ne
s — a — d
t — ow — n
ch — u — g

m — ou — se
l — a — mp
m — oo — n
p — u — ff
r — e — d
b — a — th
sh — e — d
t — e — n
b — i — ke
f — ee — t

Hearing Syllables

Share with children these common words, asking them to listen and recognize individual syllables. As children become proficient, let them try the longer words.

Note: One syllable words can sometimes be difficult because children may tend to distort them into multi-syllable words, for example, "schoo-ul" rather than "school."

One-syllable Words

ball	bat	barn	blue
boom	bounce	broke	bunch
bug	cake	cat	chug
chuck	clown	come	cool
door	dad	dime	drag
each	earth	fast	flag
flame	fly	game	good
grab	gold	green	hay
help	hop	hike	jump
jazz	ice	kick	king
kite	light	lake	lamp
maid	march	may	moon
mouse	neck	nine	old
out	pop	please	puff
pan	pack	prince	red
rust	rock	sad	school
shut	soup	slop	sure
sheet	think	town	tree

Hearing Syllables

Two-syllable Words

apple	asleep	basket	balloon
banjo	barter	because	branches
brother	carry	ceiling	children
candy	comic	crazy	danger
desert	donkey	doctor	engine
echo	elbow	flapping	forest
giraffe	gallon	garden	hungry
herself	halfway	island	jungle
kitten	landslide	little	living
meow	magnet	mammal	number
open	orange	perhaps	puzzle
parent	popcorn	quarter	rafter
robber	rooster	rusty	shouted
sorry	sudden	summer	teacher
tadpole	thousand	tiger	weather
welcome	wooden	winter	zebra

Hearing Syllables

Three-syllable Words

afternoon
animal
attention
another
beautiful
basketball
bicycle
citizen
cinnamon
companion
cucumber
dangerous
department
direction
easily
electric
elephant
fantasy
forever
gingerbread
general
gentleman
Halloween
hamburger
Joshua
kettledrum
knucklebone
library
magnetic
Kentucky
mystery
November
October
operate
outrageous
oxygen
possible
pretended
passenger
remember
seventeen
subtraction
suggested
sensitive
tablecloth
terrible
together
tomorrow
umbrella
vinegar
vacation
windowsill
woodcutter
wondering

Hearing Syllables

Four-syllable Words

adjustable	alligator	advertisement	Alabama
America	arithmetic	colonial	combination
dandelion	dictionary	exclamation	exasperate
elevator	February	grammatical	independent
January	kindergarten	Mississippi	magnificent
motorcycle	nevertheless	Oklahoma	observation
photographer	particular	rhinoceros	ridiculous
satisfaction	secretary	terrarium	Victoria

Five-syllable Words

astronomical	administration	communicable	complimentary
disagreeable	determination	exterminator	immediately
elementary	individual	international	Louisiana
multiplication	nationality	Pennsylvania	refrigerator
serendipity			

Hearing Syllables

Compound Words

afternoon	barefoot	campfire	cowboy
flowerpot	lampshade	policeman	toothpaste
crybaby	prizefighter	footprint	lawmaker
flashlight	ladybug	playground	birthday
smokestack	toothbrush	zookeeper	yourself
sidewalk	snowfall	tollbooth	washtub
airplane	barnyard	blueberry	cardboard
dustpan	eyeglass	homework	nutshell
skateboard	tiptoe	windmill	uproot
ballpark	candlestick	anywhere	cowbell
classroom	butterfly	background	carload
skyscraper	racehorse	Thanksgiving	underground
fairground	kettledrum	notebook	outfit
anything	babysit	brainstorm	chalkboard
riverboat	songwriter	supermarket	wildcat
daytime	everywhere	haystack	homesick

Hearing Syllables

Compound Words

battleship	groundhog	caretaker	bluebird
workshop	something	understand	without
strawberry	footstep	kingsize	graveyard
backstroke	beehive	bridegroom	applesauce
sunshine	yearbook	shortcut	summertime
herself	hillside	maybe	myself
wastebasket	weathervane	sunflower	railroad
outside	peanut	necktie	dishwasher
stomachache	storybook	reindeer	waterfall
farmhouse	featherweight	keyboard	pinwheel
sandbox	stepladder	surfboard	watercolor
nutcracker	indoors	haircut	gentleman
thunderstorm	wallpaper	sandpaper	starfish
darkroom	grandfather	gumdrop	lunchroom
lighthouse	goldfish	cupcake	doorbell

Picture Cards

Picture cards are a vital part of most phonemic activities. Picture cards enable children to hear sounds and recognize phonemic patterns, without yet being able to read words. They are a wonderful way to get children to listen to language and guide them to make the connection between the oral and written word.

This book includes over ten pages of picture cards. The first two pages (34–35) are for rhyming words. The remaining pages can be used for all other activities.

Strategies for implementing the picture cards

- You do not need to tear these pages out and cut the pictures apart. Reproduce the pages for children to use, leaving the master copies intact in the book.
- After reproducing a sheet of picture cards, you might glue it to oaktag or posterboard, then laminate with clear adhesive paper. This will make your cards more sturdy and longer lasting. Then cut the cards apart.
- Store the cards in envelopes. You might label one envelope "Rhyming Words," for the picture cards on pages 34–35. Keep the rest of the cards in a separate envelope.
- For pages 36–45, you might choose to keep the pages together, cut the pages into individual cards, or cut the pages into individual picture strips. You can also reproduce the pages several times to do all three.
- Tape the envelopes of picture cards on the inside and back covers of this book. The pictures will always be readily accessible when you need them.

Bingo Game

On page 46, you will find a template for a "Bingo" game card. Here is how to set up the cards:

- Reproduce several copies of the rhyming picture cards on pages 34–35.
- Randomly paste one picture card for each rhyming pair into the spaces on the game board. For example, if you paste the word *cat*, do not paste the card for *bat*. Each card should have words in different places.
- Make your own master card by gluing on the second words of the rhyming pairs—for example, *bat*.
- Laminate the boards to make them sturdier.

Hearing Sounds

As children try to distinguish and count individual sounds in words, invite them to use the activity sheet on page 47 to help them.

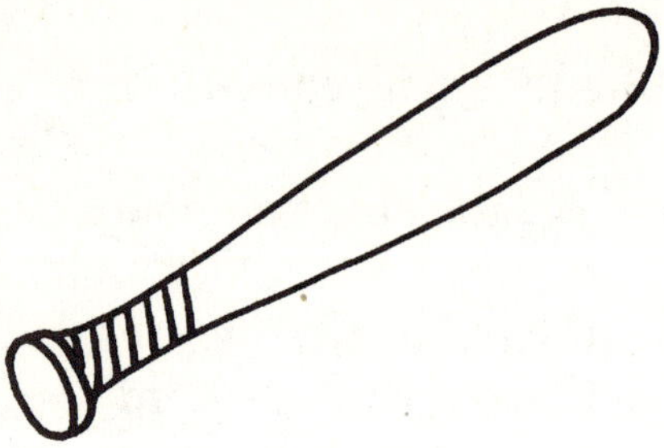

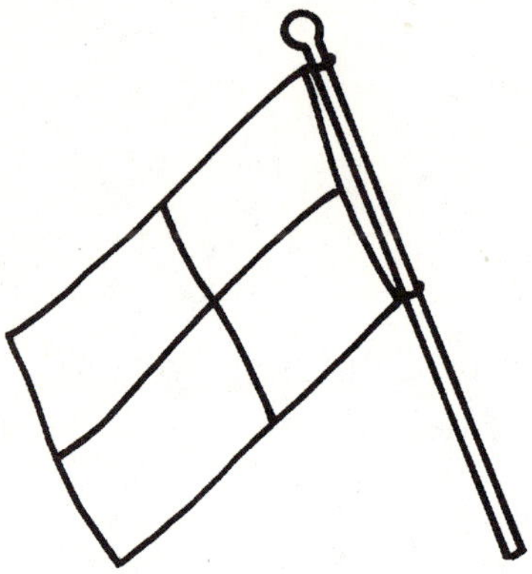

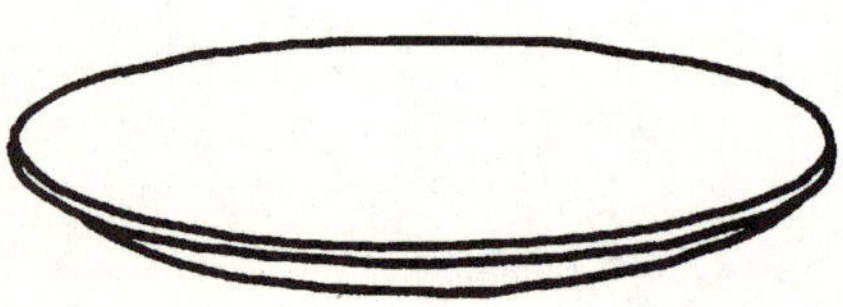

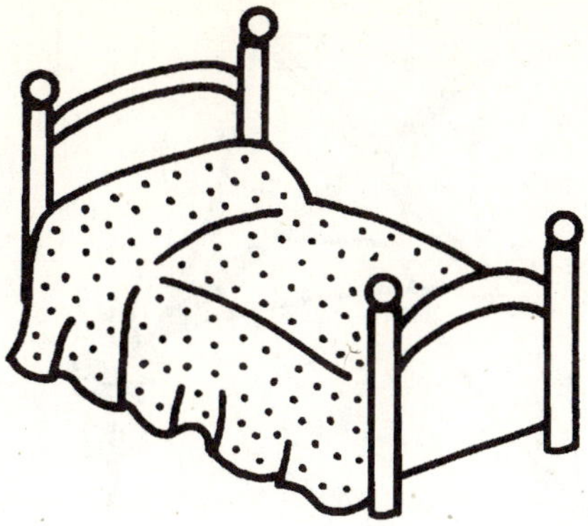
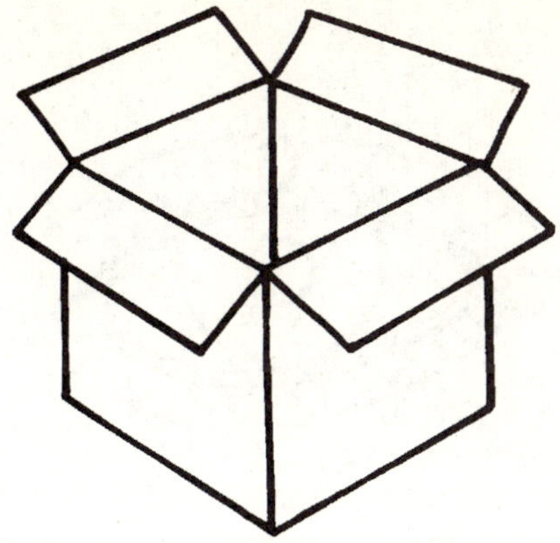

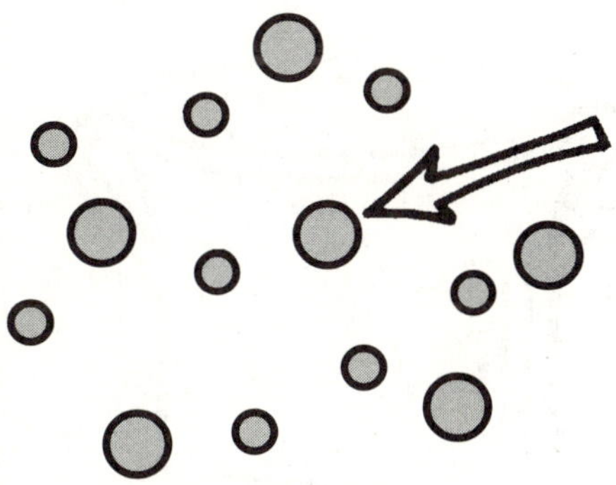
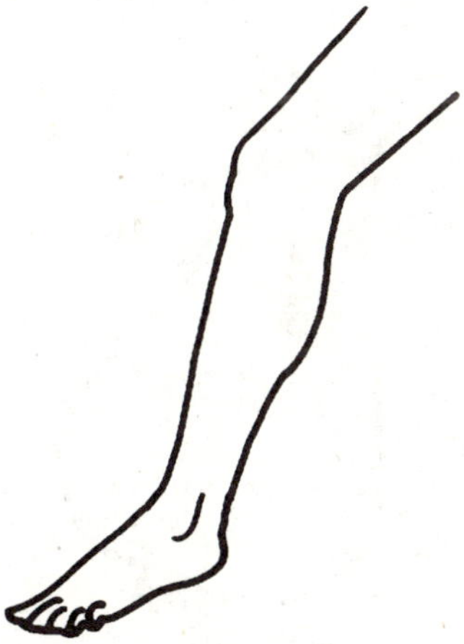
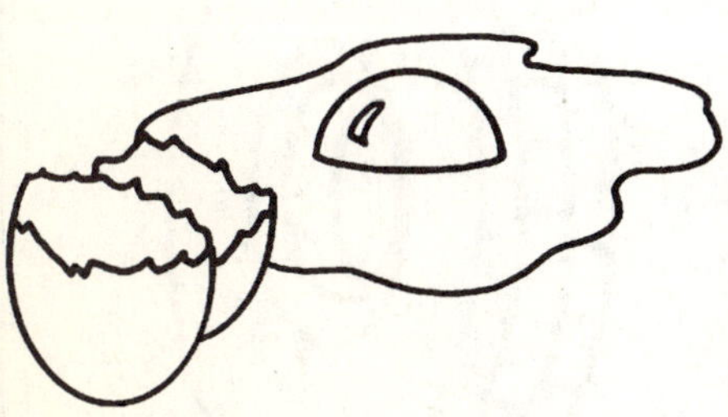
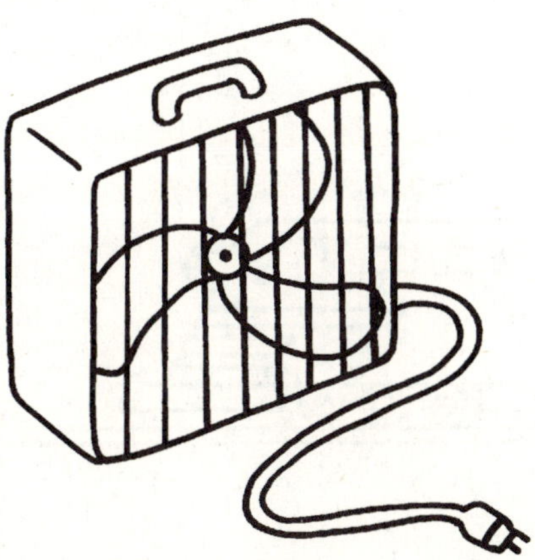

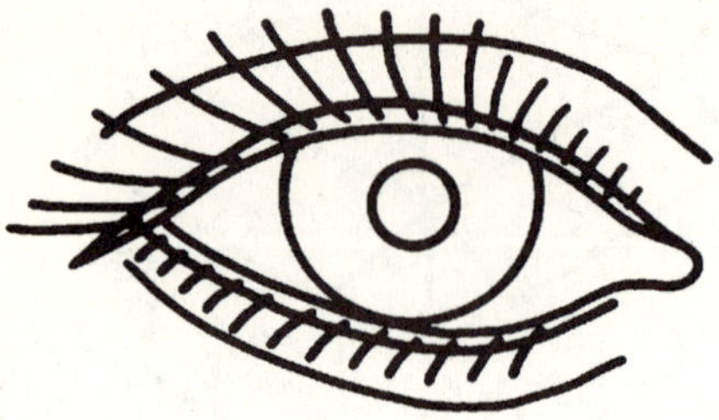
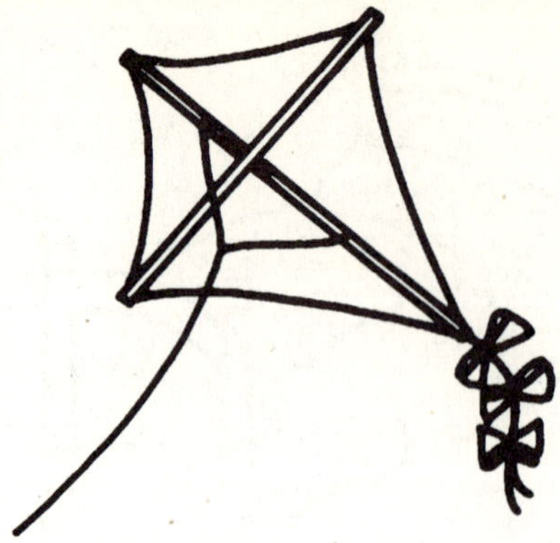
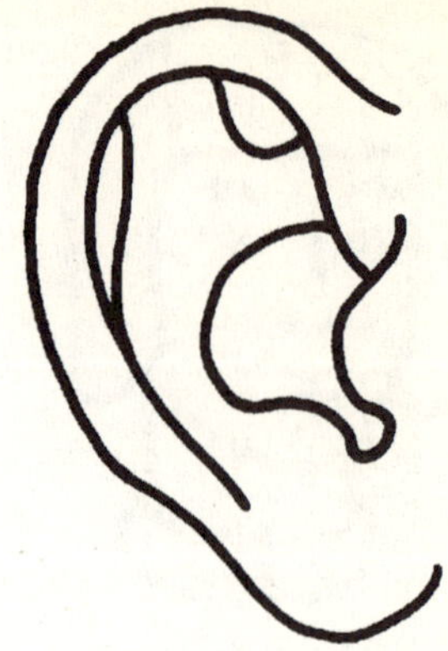

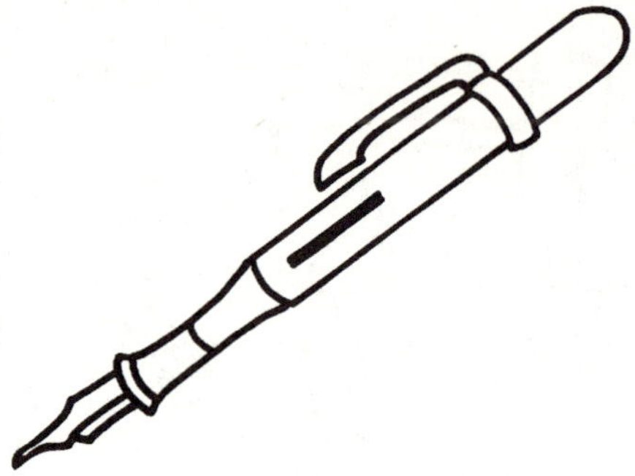

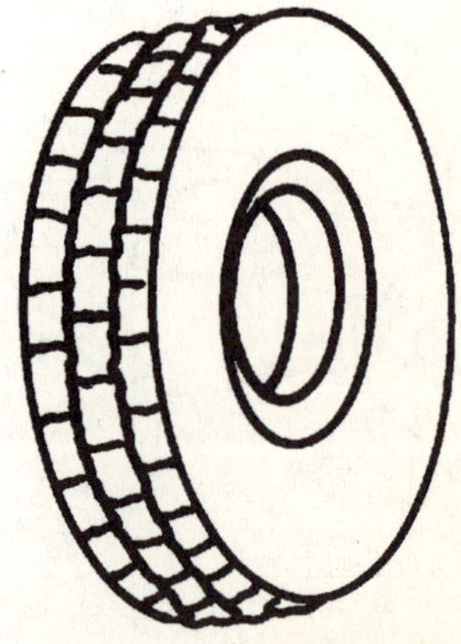

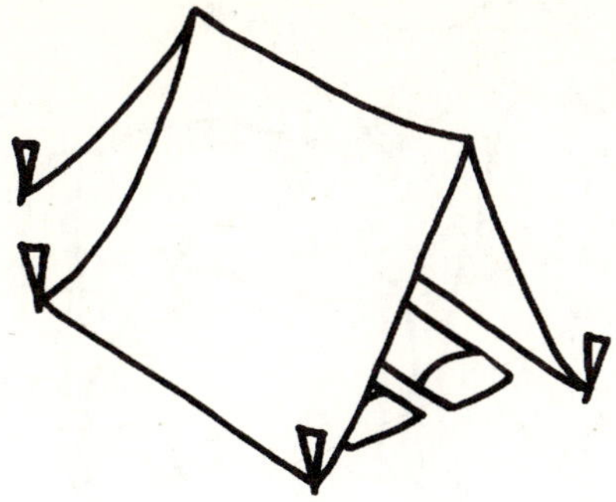

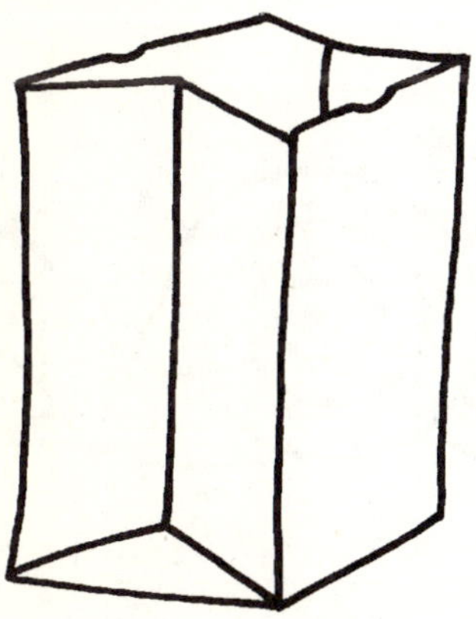

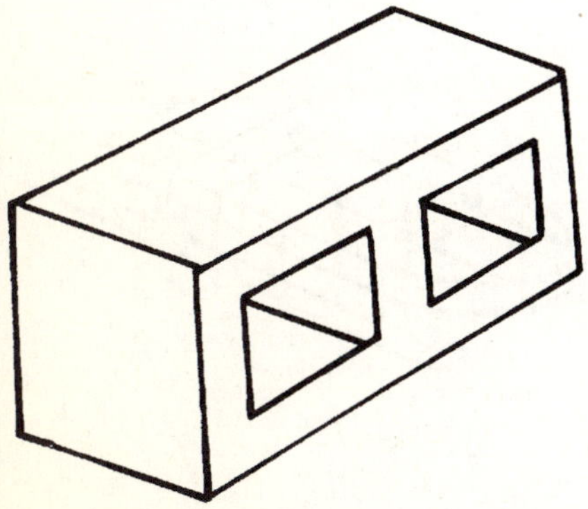
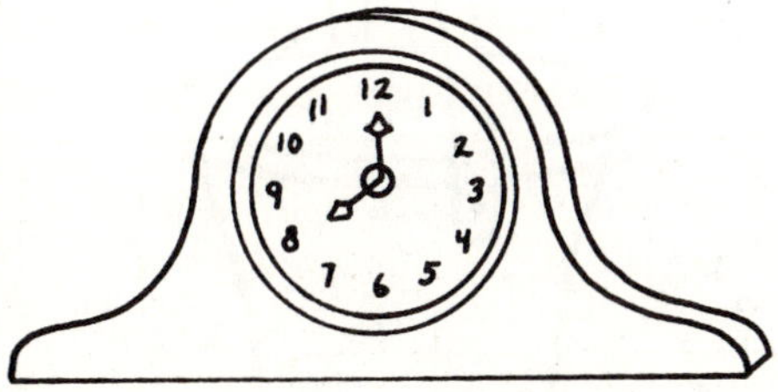

Reproducible

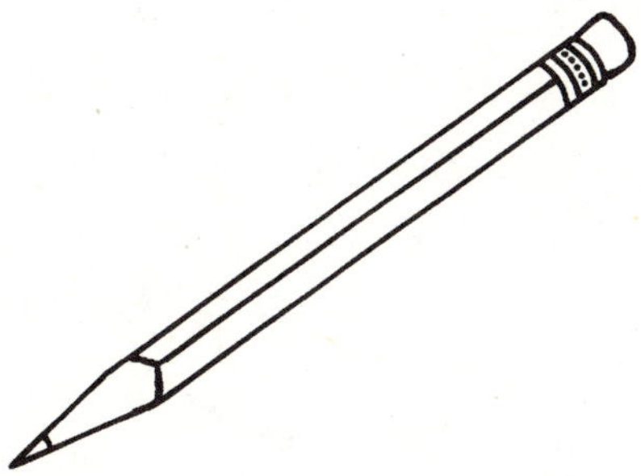

AMERICA
N
W
E
S

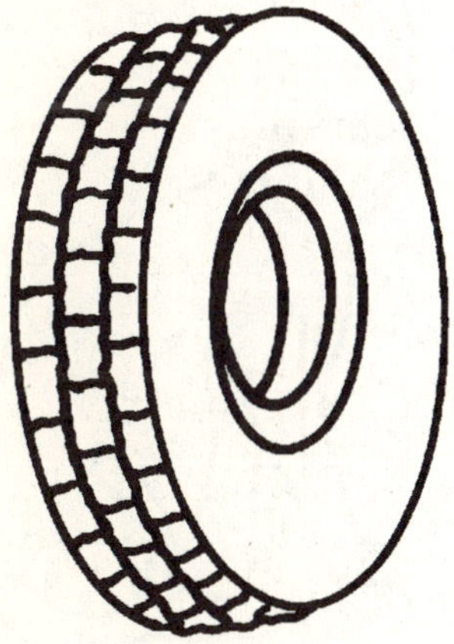
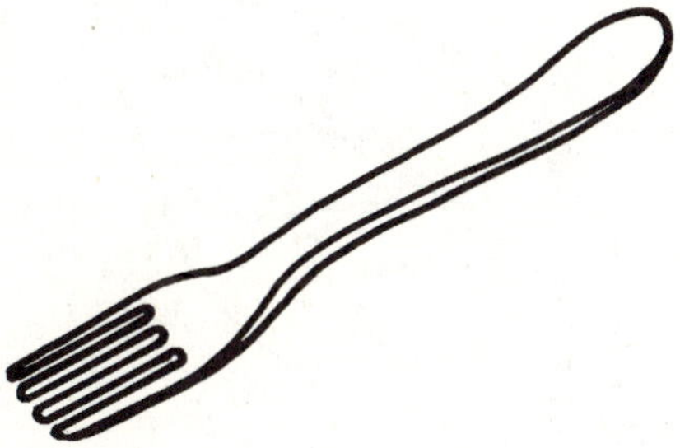

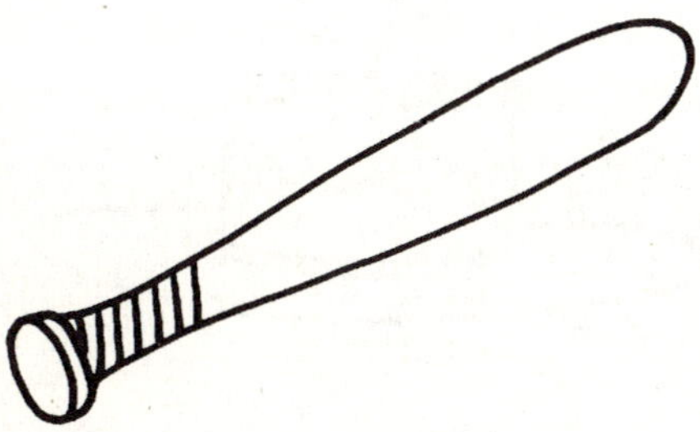
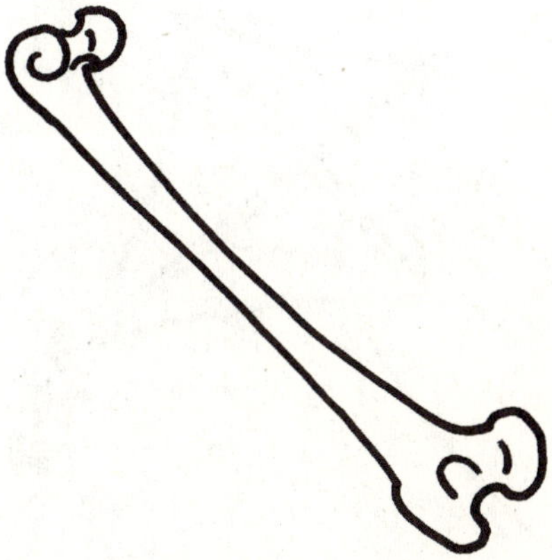

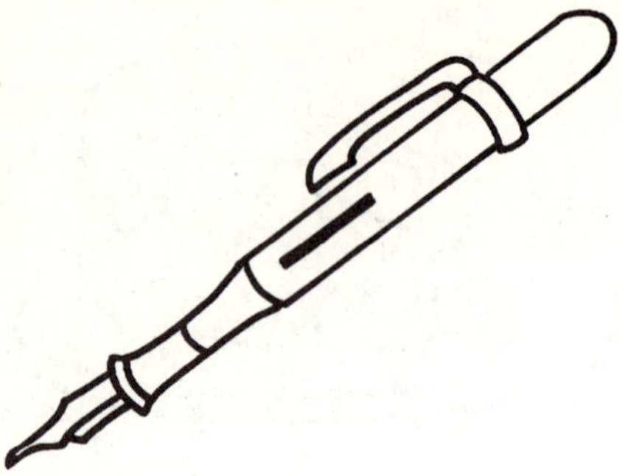

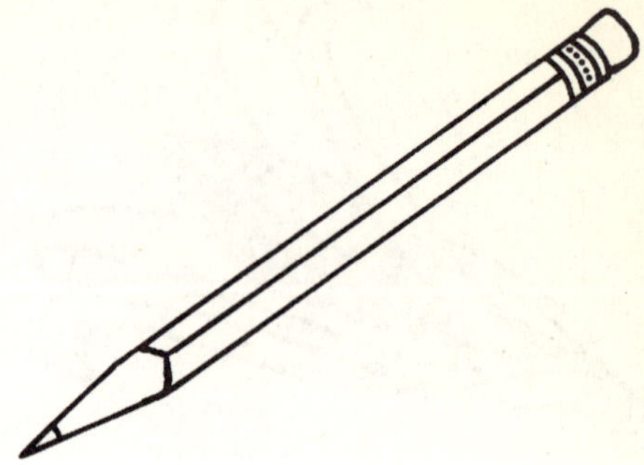

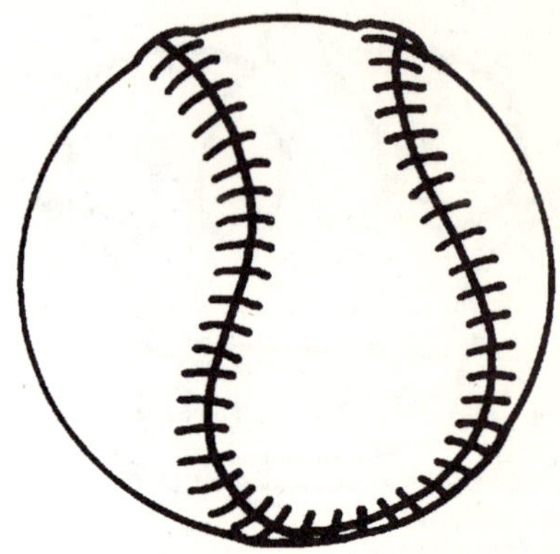
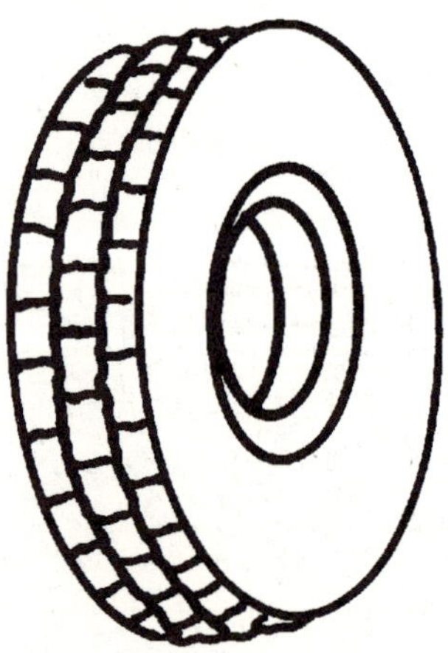

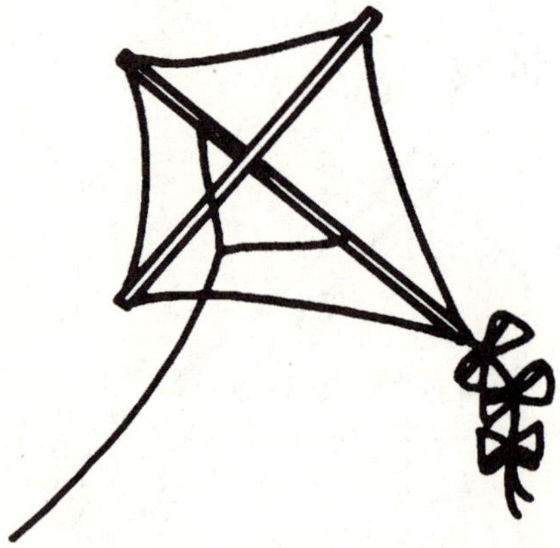

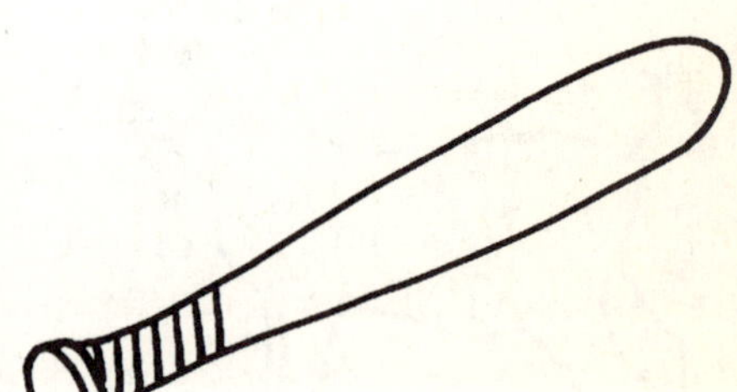

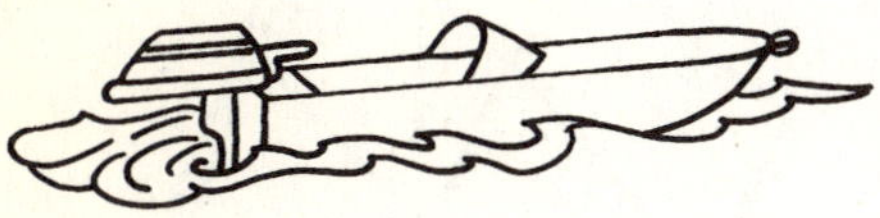

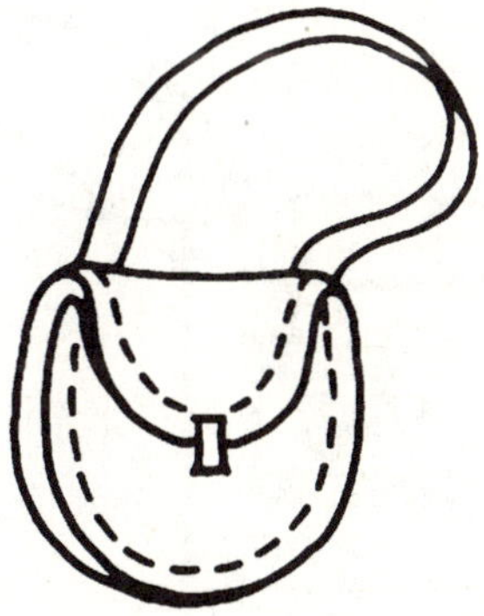

BINGO

 Reproducible

Hearing Sounds Activity Sheet

How many sounds do you hear in each word? Count all the sounds. Move a marker down the page to show how many sounds you hear.

1 Sound

2 Sounds

3 Sounds

4 Sounds

5 Sounds

Picture Card List

Rhyming Cards

Page 34	Page 36	Page 38	Page 40	Page 42	Page 44
bat	eye	house	fish	pen	can
cat	kite	horse	dish	rock	pin
bag	ear	mouth	fox	pencil	flag
flag	fly	mouse	brush	ten	bag
duck	pen	wagon	star	fire	fork
truck	hen	whistle	stair	ball	ant
goat	pear	window	jar	tire	can
coat	pot	dragon	moon	leaf	hanger
fish	truck	snail	towel	cat	house
dish	duck	snake	turkey	kite	horse
mouse	train	pail	owl	hat	rat
house	tire	sled	turtle	bat	three

Rhyming Cards

Page 35	Page 37	Page 39	Page 41	Page 43	Page 45
head	top	cat	corn	boat	eight
bed	tent	can	horn	house	tree
box	doll	hat	cake	coat	boat
fox	mop	coat	crown	goat	house
hen	sock	pail	fire	pie	coat
men	shoe	pot	tie	tie	goat
pot	bag	file	tire	fish	pie
dot	lock	pencil	fork	fly	tie
leg	sock	hat	boat	purse	fish
egg	block	car	goat	pig	five
fan	clock	cup	bat	nurse	hive
man	dish	map	bone	man	six